BOLD KIDS

CHILDREN'S BOOK WITH INTRIGUING INFORMATIVE FACTS

No part of this book may be reproduced or used in any way or form or by any means whether electronic or mechanical, this means that you cannot record or photocopy any material ideas or tips that are provided in this book.
Copyright 2022

All images in this book have been reproduced with the knowledge and prior consent of the artists concerned, and no responsibility is accepted by producer, publisher, or printer for any infringement of copyright or otherwise, arising from the contents of this publication.

Fun Facts about Venus for Kids: This planet is very similar to Earth, but it is very different, too. For one thing, a day on Venus is longer than a year. A day is the length of time it takes a planet to revolve on its axis.

For example, it takes 225 Earth days to orbit the sun. If you were to travel to Venus by spacecraft, you would have to fly around for ten days to do so.

There are six mountain regions on Venus. These mountain ranges range in size from about 0.5 to 150 miles across. Lava flows can also create long canals that are more than 3,000 miles long.

This makes Venus one of the longest lava flows of any planet. In fact, the planet has more volcanoes than any other planet. While it takes 225 Earth days to orbit the sun, it takes only 117 Venusian days to rotate around the sun.

Another fact about Venus that many children don't know is that it is cloudy. Like Earth, Venus is constantly covered in clouds. The clouds are made of carbon dioxide, and their greenhouse effect traps heat, making the planet the hottest of the solar system.

This is also what makes it such an interesting planet for kids to study. The moon of the sun, Mercury, is the closest to the Sun. The two planets are almost identical in size, and the differences in composition make them interesting for both adults and children.

Aside from being the second brightest object in the night sky, Venus is so far away that you can't see it during transit of the sun. It is also the only planet in our solar system that has a moon, making it the perfect place for children to learn about the planet.

Its atmosphere is filled with sulfuric acid, which traps heat and makes it an ideal destination for astronauts. However, Venus isn't as lovable as the other planets in the solar system, and it is not a candidate for a mate.

The planet Venus is a little smaller than Earth, but it is still very similar in terms of density, mass, and gravity. It also has a thick atmosphere made of carbon dioxide and yellowish sulfuric acid clouds. Unlike Earth, it doesn't have moons or rings.

As the second planet from the Sun, it is far away from the Earth. Its sun is opposite that of Earth. If you were to visit Venus, it would take 117 Earth days to travel a mile in one direction.

The planet Venus has a thick atmosphere. The top layer is the cloud bank, while the bottom layer is the rest of the planet. In fact, the atmosphere of Venus is composed of three distinct layers: the surface, the ozone layer, and the clouds.

The first one is the hottest, the second is the coldest, and the third is the most humid. But when you travel to Venus, you can learn a lot about its different climates.

Venus has two broad layers of atmosphere. The upper layer is made of clouds, while the lower layer is the planet's atmosphere. It's the cloud bank that makes the planet's atmosphere so thick.

In the past, people thought Venus was a hot planet. Today, however, Venus is the only planet with clouds, so it's not too hot, either. For this reason, it's impossible to live on the surface of Venus.

While Venus is bright and easy to see, it isn't as friendly as we might expect. Its surface is covered with thick clouds that cover the planet, and it looks much like Earth at dusk. A day on Venus is the equivalent of 117 Earth days.

It is a red planet, so its brightness can be attributed to its slow rotation. The brightness of Venus is also a result of the fact that the planet is different from the other planets.

The planet Venus is a little smaller than Earth, but its mass and density are very similar. Its gravity is similar to that of Earth. The planet is not a magnet, which is why it is called "love" on the other planets. The planet also has a magnetic field.

This magnetic field is important to the planet's atmosphere. In addition to the magnetic field, the atmosphere of Venus contains large amounts of carbon dioxide. The high concentration of carbon dioxide creates an intense greenhouse effect, trapping heat in the atmosphere.

Lightning Source UK Ltd.
Milton Keynes UK
UKHW051917100922
408607UK00005B/145

9 781071 712122